TV STUDIO

Library Edition Published 1990

© Cherrytree Press Ltd 1989
© Marshall Cavendish Limited 1990

Library Edition produced by DPM Services Limited

Printed in Italy

Library of Congress Cataloging-in-Publication Data

Graham, Alison.
  T.V. studio / by Alison Graham
    p. cm. – (Lets go to)
  Includes index.
  Summary: Describes, in simple text and illustrations, a television studio and how a show is prepared.
  ISBN 1-85435-244-X
  1. Television – Production and direction – Juvenile literature. [1. Television – Production and direction.] I. Title. II. Series: Graham, Alison.
Lets go to.
  PN1992.75.G74 1990
  791.45'023 – dc20
                                       89-22046
                                           CIP
                                           AC

Let's Go To a
TV STUDIO

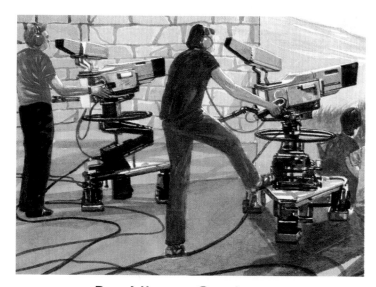

By Alison Graham
Illustrated by Nik Spender

MARSHALL CAVENDISH
New York · London · Toronto · Sydney

What do you like watching on the television? Do you like football? Do you like quiz shows? Do you like the news? Do you ever wonder how all these different programs get onto the screen? Let's go to a TV station and find out.

At the TV station, they are about to put on a play about pirates. We meet the producer of the program. He shows us the studio where the play is to be filmed.

There are several other studios at the TV station. A quiz show is being broadcast from one of them. The news is being shown in another.

news

soccer

drama

The director tells us what has happened so far to get the play ready. He has chosen a technical director and a team of helpers. Each person has a special job.

The scriptwriter has written the screenplay. It tells the actors what to do and say.

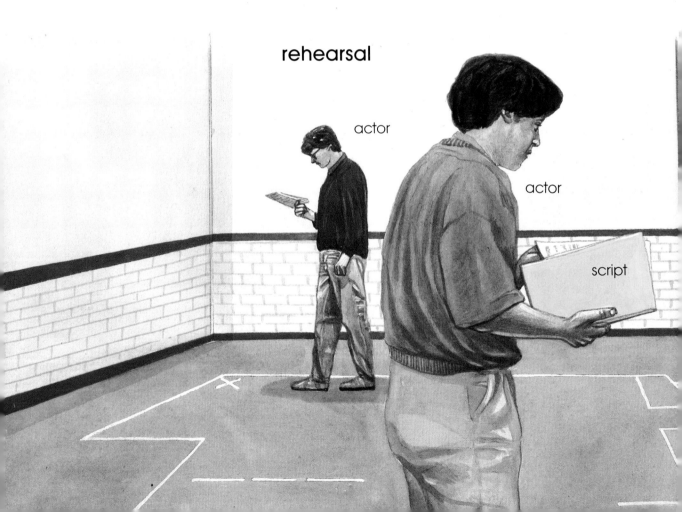

rehearsal

actor

actor

script

The director has chosen the actors. The actors in a play arc callcd the cast. They all have a copy of the words they have to say. It is called the script.

All the cast have to learn their lines from the script. Then they rehearse them all together.

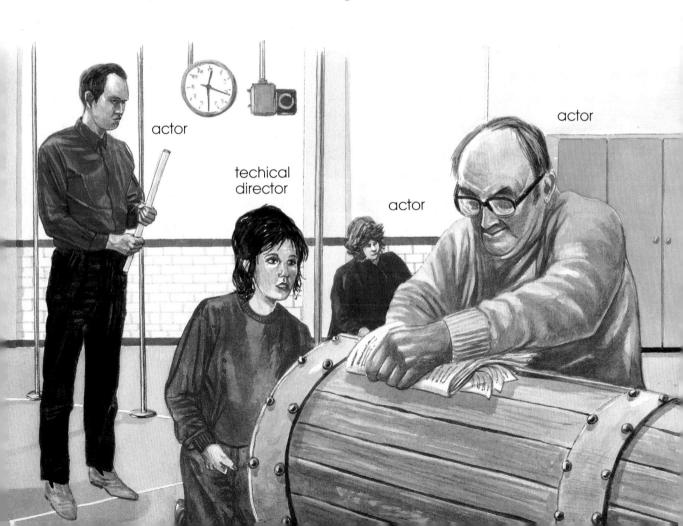

actor

techical director

actor

actor

building sets

carpenters

The play takes place on a ship. The ship has to be made in the studio.

The art director and her helpers make the scenery from wood and plastic, and paint it to look real. They do not build a whole ship, just parts of one.

art director

The scenery is called a set. Several sets are needed for the play. One shows the deck of the ship. One shows a harbor. One shows a dungeon. Most of the sets show off the sea as well.

The special effects department is making a giant octopus.

wardrobe

costume designer

actor

wardrobe

The actors in the play have to wear costumes. Sometimes, the costumes for a play are rented. For this play, most of them have been specially designed.

The costume designer and the wardrobe department make sure that the costumes fit the actors.

10

Other things are needed, too – old tables and lamps,
drinking cups and bowls, guns, swords, treasure
chests, and lots of treasure. All these things are called
properties, or props.

The play is a true story, so all the details have to be
correct. The properties must all look as if they come
from the right time in history.

props

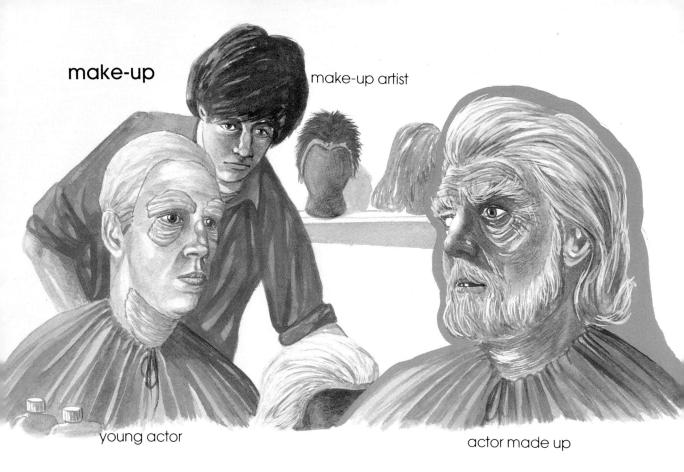

make-up

make-up artist

young actor

actor made up

The actors have to wear make-up for the cameras.
One of the actors has to look very old. The make-up
artist puts plastic pads under his eyes to make them
look baggy. He uses spirit gum to make the actor's
skin look wrinkly. He gives him a wig of long white hair
and a false beard and eyebrows. He blackens some
of his teeth to make them look as if they are missing.

12

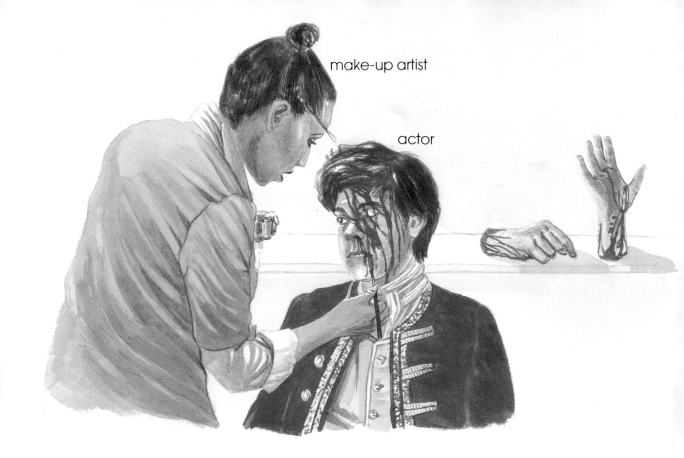

make-up artist

actor

Another character is wounded in a fight in the play. Before the fight, he must look normal. Afterward, he has to have artificial cuts and bruises. He must be dripping with fake blood.

A model is made of the actor's hand. It looks as if it has been cut off in the play.

13

When the sets and costumes are ready, the actors rehearse on the set.

The camera crew comes to the rehearsals. They need to see what they have to film. Lighting engineers come to plan the lighting. They have to make some scenes sunny, some moonlit.

camera rehearsal

camera operator

Audio engineers come, too. They make sure that the microphones are in the right places to pick up the sound.

Special effects people plan the music and sound effects. They also have to figure out how to show the pirate ship sinking at the end of the play.

audio engineer

lighting engineer

camera operator

The play is ready to be filmed. The actors know their parts and their moves. The sets, props, costumes, and make-up are all perfect. Now the director has to make sure that everything is technically all right.

The play is filmed scene by scene – but maybe not in the right order. Filming is called shooting. As one scene is being shot, another is being made ready.

actor

stage
hand

preparing the set

The stage manager is in charge of the studio. There are three production assistants. One tells the actors when to come onto the set. One dircts the lighting. One directs the stage hands. There are lots of stage hands. They move the scenery and props.

Everyone is very quiet, because the studio is "live." Every sound is recorded.

stage
manager

live studio

production
assistants

cameras

There are three cameras in the studio. Each one sees the scene from a different height or angle. Each one produces a different view of the scene.

Cameras have to move quickly and silently. Some are on wheels, so that the operator can push them into position. The cameras can move up and down and swivel.

camera boom

boom microphone

One of the cameras is on a boom. It can be swung around in an arc. The camera operator can sit high up and look down on the scene. He can move the camera from side to side. This is called panning.

The camera can be moved sideways very quickly. It can keep pace with someone running. A microphone on a boom keeps pace with the camera.

lights

microphone

camera

production assistant

High above the studio floor are hundreds of lights. They are attached to rails and can be moved around. These powerful lights flood the scene being filmed. They give a bright, clear picture.

Microphones pick up the sound. Some are on booms that move. They are held over the actors' heads, out of sight of the cameras. Others are hidden on the set. If the actors are moving around a lot, they have tiny microphones clipped to their clothes.

The microphones pick up every sound, so everyone in the studio wears soft shoes.

close-up picture

headphone

The camera crew all wear headphones. The technical director can talk to them from the control room. She tells them when and where to move their cameras.

All the cameras have zoom lenses. They take close-up pictures. The camera has a small screen. On it, the operator can see what he is shooting. He can make sure that there are no wires or stage hands in the picture!

Each camera is connected by cable to the control room. Whatever a camera is filming appears on a television screen called a monitor.

The director looks at all the monitors. He decides which picture to show on the screen when the play is shown on the television.

An editor makes sure that each scene merges into the next in a natural way.

control room

sound control room

The microphones are also connected to a control room. The audio engineers raise or lower the level of sound from the microphones.

They mix in special effects, like the sound of waves. They make the guns sound as if they are really firing. They make the splashing noise when people fall in the water. They make the crashing noise when people break chairs over each other's heads.

24

Other effects are created by the special effects department. They can make plastic that looks like glass. It breaks without hurting anyone. They make swords that do no harm.

They use plastic foam to make great thick walls. They use light balsa wood to make furniture that looks solid. It smashes easily in a fight. The stuntmen have to pretend that they are being hurt.

stuntman

actor

stuntman

special effects

During the play, ships are shown at sea. The ships are not filmed on the sea. They are small models filmed in the studio. A film of waves and clouds rushing by is played onto a screen.

In front of the screen, the model ship is rocked up and down. The camera shoots the model and the screen. On the television, it looks as if the ship is really sailing.

The pirate ship in the play is set on fire. They cannot burn the set. Instead, they make a model of the ship from putty, cardboard, and cotton. They make it look as if it is on fire with chemical flames.

The little model is placed in a tank of real water. As it burns, it sinks below the waves. Through the camera, it looks as if a real ship is sinking.

newsroom

autocue
operator

newscaster

The play is finished. It is time for us to go home. Before we go, the director shows us some of the other studios at the television station.

In one, they are broadcasting the news. The news is shown live. Everyone has to be careful not to make mistakes. The newscaster sees the words he is to say on a teleprompter. He listens to his producer through a tiny earphone.

The director gives us a Fact File which answers lots of our questions. Our play has been recorded on videotape. Before it is shown, the editors will cut out any mistakes. They will make sure that the play runs for exactly the right length of time.

It is very exciting watching the play on the television. It took many weeks to make, and only one hour to show.

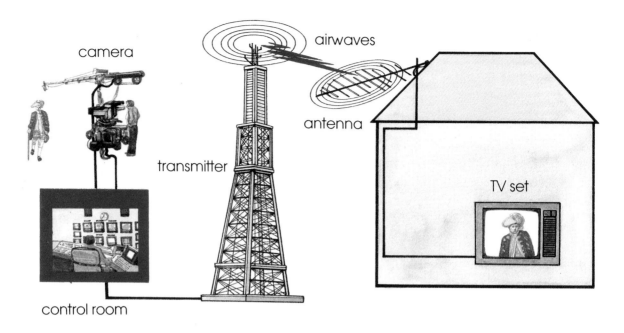

camera

airwaves

transmitter

antenna

TV set

control room

Fact File

How does the television picture reach the screen?

The TV camera turns the picture it sees into an electrical signal. This signal goes to a transmitter. The transmitter is a tall tower. It sends out a signal on invisible waves in the air. The signals are picked up by the antenna on your house. The antenna goes to the TV set. The signals are turned back into a picture by the set.

How are programs made away from TV studios?

For small events, only one camera is needed. A single video camera is enough to film an interview with someone. For a football game, the television company uses a mobile studio. There are several cameras that follow the play. The program is transmitted back to the studio by air or by cable. The director, audio engineers, and vision controllers work inside a trailer. Viewers can see the game as it is taking place. Broadcasts made away from the studios are called outside broadcasts.

What is satellite television?
Lots of television programs are relayed by satellites. The signal from the transmitter goes up into space. It is picked up by a satellite and sent to another part of the world. Private television stations have their own satellites. People with satellite dishes on their homes can pick up the signals straight from the satellites.

What is cable television?
Cable television stations send signals from the transmitter by cable. Each house with cable television is linked to a larger cable carrying the signal. You do not need a dish to receive cable television.

What is closed-circuit television?
A closed circuit is a private television system. Shops and banks use hidden cameras that watch the customers. Security staff watch on monitor screens. They can see if anyone shoplifts or tries to rob the bank.

outside broadcast

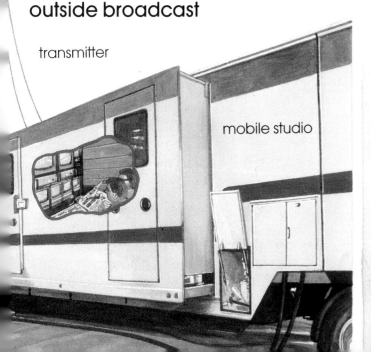

transmitter

mobile studio

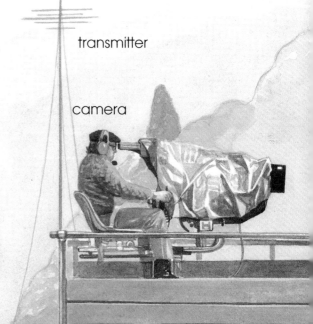

transmitter

camera

Index